Life
lessons
through loss,
learning
and love

Life lessons through loss, learning and love

TRACY S. GALLAGHER

Archway Publishing books may be ordered through booksellers or by contacting:

Archway Publishing
1663 Liberty Drive
Bloomington, IN 47403
www.archwaypublishing.com
844-669-3957

ISBN: 978-1-6657-7041-5 (sc)
ISBN: 978-1-6657-7042-2 (e)

Library of Congress Control Number: 2024926394

Print information available on the last page.

Archway Publishing rev. date: 01/03/2025

Contents

A day away

Time is moving so quickly through our children's young lives that one day, it seems, they have become adults overnight. If we could take some time out of each day to pause and see these incredible lives as they stand before us. Their minds are sponges taking in every nuance of your time together. Be mindful that the time is filled with tenderness and love for roads ahead. Not every moment of life together will be absent of worry or pain. How you move through these moments will guide them to a place where they will feel confident that they can master their future struggles.

Family

When we walk a path in life together,
we walk in many different shoes.
When we share life with others,
we take on different viewpoints.
Children raised in the same household,
will see variations of the same situation.
A point to be remembered,
when dealing with others in life.

Reality

If I am with you,
do you really see me?
If I speak with you,
are you really listening?
When we lose focus with others,
we are not sharing time together.
It's important for you to be present,
respect the others importance.
If the encounter is not real,
its time wasted.

Breathe

It's time to give yourself a break,
allow yourself to take a moment to just breathe.
Don't think about the obligations knocking you
down or the deadlines interfering with your
thoughts. Just stop and give yourself a much-needed
hug. Life will be okay for a moment without
you.

Today

Today your pathways may seem improbable to navigate, trust in yourself to find the best way. Many paths of uncertainty will help you gain the necessary skills toward your journey.

Find your path

If ever we seem to get off track, remember that we are still able to move forward. It is during these moments that we will gain the knowledge needed for the tomorrows which were previously lacking in clarity of purpose.

The roads ahead

Today I will step back so I can gain a clearer view of
what lies before me. Some roads may be shrouded
in darkness making the journey much harder to see.
You know what you know, trust in that.

Be open

I feel an emptiness for the day was void of any
meaning. Each day I wake, I try to take notice of
others who may be hiding the pain of life inside.
I cannot change some, for the tears run too deep,
while others will accept the hand of another. It is not
always about the journey for those facing such pain,
but the willingness to take the challenge.

By extension

Today I am feeling a sadness within my heart for so much I do not know. Each space I enter is another challenge to understand why I take on the feelings of others. This burden by extension can be very painful because I do not have the understanding or awareness of where my heartache is coming from. I am grateful, however, for the ability to hear others without a voice to hide behind.

Light

Allow yourself the light in times of darkness. Any path you are facing is much harder to see if you will not accept your inner strength. Take heed in the journey for which you were chosen to follow. Others will also benefit from the lessons gained. For each of us it is only a small part of a greater whole. Do not take less than is needed, never take more than is necessary. Find peace in your balance.

Remembering

As a child I appreciated her nature and life. She seldom gave into such odious acts that demeaned others. She did not make notice of secrets they may be trying to hide from her. She would only see the good in their effort to overcome the struggles they may be facing. As we both aged, I often feared for the day when I would walk alone. She was calm in my spirit that usually ran wild. She offered only what was needed and was near for those moments I strayed too far. Some people we share our lives with will share lessons of the mind, she was a teacher of the heart. The day we took our last walk together seemed so ordinary. I take comfort in knowing that our time together was incredibly special. I will cherish my memories with her as I navigate through my own journey in a grandparent's love.

She stood beside me

Her nature was open and offered a feeling of peace
just standing beside her. She had a way about her
that attracted others to her. Her eyes could feel some
of your deepest secrets but would never ask of those
things that did not belong to her. Yesterday as she
walked along with her many years on this earth, she
allowed only a few to know the truest self. Her life
was a gift to some and a mystery to others.

Reflection

When we decide to judge others with eyes of
ignorance, we block our ability to see the reflection
we embrace within ourselves.

Setbacks

Each disappointment may take you down a path of self-destruction. Tunnel vision takes over and all you can see are the distractions in your life. Setbacks are challenges you may not be ready for. When we only see the negative, we will miss all the positive steps you have taken thus far. It is hard sometimes to get out of a spiral of negativity when every day seems to only bring you more disappointment. When we can take a step back and mindful of the entire picture, we will see the positive steps. Even though they may not seem memorable they are still important to your overall faith in not giving up. Give yourself a break and applaud yourself for the wins while learning from the losses.

Work

When we avoid taking time off work because we feel guilty, we are doing ourselves a disservice. Work can be a necessary part of our lives, and we need to keep the overall picture in perspective. Work, although a big part of life, is only a means to an end. For some their work is their life, taking time to reset is always needed no matter the investment. There are few prolonged activities that are more demanding of your time than the hours put into work. It is for that very reason that we must allow ourselves to take time away. Burnout is a reality because we or others we allow are pushing too hard.

Change

People who are bent on self-destruction will only pull others in. The willingness to change such a cycle isn't for others to do, it is solely upon the individual to see what is happening and change those things. When bad things happen to us, we try to prevent others from having to endure a similar experience. In so doing, we jump in to help others flailing along with what seems no direction. Sometimes no direction for them is what is comfortable. Life isn't always fair, or equally divided. Those who prosper from a time of great pain are those who use the lessons learned and don't let the same keep them from moving on. Be open to kindness for others, but don't become an enabler to one who may not really want to change.

Yesterday's friendship

When someone close to you has betrayed you
in such a way that it ends a relationship, it is
devastating. This person, in your eyes, was a part
of your yesterday's and within the stitching of your
tomorrows. Many of the memories of your life
involved this person. It's hard to move on when your
future was safely locked and loaded on the next phase
of your life. It is hard, but certainly not impossible to
find a new path making new memories. Our hearts
are resilient, healing itself from some of the worst
moments in life. Don't carry the hurt of the betrayal
with you, let it go, you have a new life waiting
for you.

Cries of the heart

When the heart cries out for something to hold onto
how can you give it hope. When life just can't seem
to let go of some places where do you go to find
answers?

Travel

As we travel through life, sometimes the path before
us becomes narrow with the uncertainty of which
direction to take. Nothing in life is certain. It's only
the hope that what we believe we see will be the most
beneficial for us. Moments when we feel we are truly
lost, is the time to pause allowing the mind to rest
and find itself. Decisions are not destinies for anyone
to abide by just choices for what may be a resolve.
One can always change course if the road taken is
not beneficial to the goal that you had intended.

Steps to walk

Today you may want to guide another's path from a time not quite forgotten. Although you have traveled on a similar path, very few have traveled the same. It is important that you are mindful of those seeking peace. They are coming to you with the burdens of many years that they have tried to hide. It is not for others to unpack those demons without understanding the power behind the secrets. Being a friend and listening to heartache while offering support is sometimes the only thing you can do. Changing a course, you may be unfamiliar with could have lasting effects. Although we want to help, we can only be the temporary handrail for those who must find their own resolution through these inner secrets.

Judgement

Those who have the willingness not to pass
judgement upon others are rare. When meeting
others we should see them as a blank slate.
A beginning for us to fill in a portrait of the
information we are offered. When we engage with
others with prejudice, it is only ourselves who we
are seeing. We should allow ourselves to come into
relationships without the intrusion of predetermined
beliefs. The ties that we hold are those of our own
acceptance and should not be projected onto others.
It is then that we will benefit from the interactions
with a truer and more honest encounter. The
ability to listen is a much better alternative from the
intrusion of one's ego.

Apology

When we have wronged another, it is important to
be humble and correct the error. Life unfortunately
allows us to experience times when we make
missteps and hurt the ones around us. In a world
of constant change, we are bound to make a few
mistakes along the way. It is important to offer an
apology for the mistake that has been made. When
we make such a gesture it is important that we
understand the meaning of the apology. A heartfelt
apology should be freely given, allowing the other
person to accept it or not. If an apology is to
relinquish one's feelings of guilt, it is given with no
significance. Without meaning this issue will linger
in both until a resolve is rendered. It's best to just
accept the misstep and move on.

Old baggage

So many opinions are based solely on our acceptance
of words or beliefs passed on through time. Children
are open and kind without hesitation. The lessons
in life have not invaded their view of people. Due to
their limited experience thus far, they rely heavily
on adults to explain the world around them. It is
important that they can experience life anew and not
carry old experiences. As they mature, they absorb
more knowledge, allowing them to shape the person
who they want to be. I ponder sometimes of how
much of the past knowledge is revisited or just stored
in the memory. Those who guide us into maturity
are critical for our growth but can also hinder us
from having true encounters with others based upon
an old belief. Be mindful of influences, do not judge
before being shown a reason.

Today

Today your pathways may seem improbable to navigate, trust in yourself to find the best way. Many paths of uncertainty will help you gain the necessary skills toward your journey.

Find your path

If ever we seem to get off track, remember that we are still able to move forward. It is during these moments that we will gain the knowledge needed for the tomorrows which were previously lacking in clarity of purpose.

The roads ahead

Today I will step back so I can gain a clearer view of
what lies before me. Some roads may be shrouded
in darkness making the journey much harder to see.
You know what you know, trust in that.

Be open

I feel an emptiness for the day was void of any
meaning. Each day I wake, I try to take notice of
others who may be hiding the pain of life inside.
I cannot change some, for the tears run too deep,
while others will accept the hand of another. It is not
always about the journey for those facing such pain,
but the willingness to take the challenge.

By extension

Today I am feeling a sadness within my heart for so much I do not know. Each space I enter is another challenge to understand why I take on the feelings of others. This burden by extension can be very painful because I do not have the understanding or awareness of where my heartache is coming from. I am grateful, however, for the ability to hear others without a voice to hide behind.

Light

Allow yourself the light in times of darkness. Any path you are facing is much harder to see if you will not accept your inner strength. Take heed in the journey for which you were chosen to follow. Others will also benefit from the lessons gained. For each of us it is only a small part of a greater whole. Do not take less than is needed, never take more than is necessary. Find peace in your balance.

Remembering

As a child I appreciated her nature and life. She seldom gave into such odious acts that demeaned others. She did not make notice of secrets they may be trying to hide from her. She would only see the good in their effort to overcome the struggles they may be facing. As we both aged, I often feared for the day when I would walk alone. She was calm in my spirit that usually ran wild. She offered only what was needed and was near for those moments I strayed too far. Some people we share our lives with will share lessons of the mind, she was a teacher of the heart. The day we took our last walk together seemed so ordinary. I take comfort in knowing that our time together was incredibly special. I will cherish my memories with her as I navigate through my own journey in a grandparent's love.

She stood beside me

Her nature was open and offered a feeling of peace just standing beside her. She had a way about her that attracted others to her. Her eyes could feel some of your deepest secrets but would never ask of those things that did not belong to her. Yesterday as she walked along with her many years on this earth, she allowed only a few to know the truest self. Her life was a gift to some and a mystery to others.

Reflection

When we decide to judge others with eyes of
ignorance, we block our ability to see the reflection
we embrace within ourselves.

Yesterday

I feel sad for a friend I once knew but now is gone.
It was a relationship I just knew how the other was
feeling. I miss being a part of someone who just
understood my silence. Being so alone in a world
where your number rarely gets noticed can be
isolating. It is true that times like these are difficult
to get through and it must be done.

Heart

My heart is in pain for the one I have said goodbye to. Sometimes as painful as it is, the best thing to do is to walk away. The pain beckons you to give in and go back to avoid the hurt anymore. Yet it is the heart that has been broken many times before. Life is all about the gifts we get and give. If our love is lost it is best to give yourself the strength to let it find its own place.

Parents

As a parent you try to be the foundation for this life
you have brought into this world. There will be many
lessons for them to learn as they move about the
landscape of life. In some rare cases the road through
life takes a turn no one expected and this child of
yours is now a lost soul. You will begin an endless
search for one who does not want to be found. It is
a hard and lonely time for those involved. As parents
the longing and hope never fades as the search
goes on.

Forgotten days

She searches for the happiness that eludes her.
Her tears of a time she feels but cannot remember.
Recognizing within her moments of anguish for a
memory she only vaguely understands. Why is it so
that she must carry such a burden for things that
happened when she was only a child?

Continuum

When she cries, who is there to hear her pain? When she wants to give up and end this continuum of pain, who is there to show her another way? Life for some individuals is one heartache after another. There are no more places to hide and no one to run to.

Dreams

Do not give the shadows that visit your dreams time
to become a part of your inner peace. Moments
of pain will open you up to feel or see images of
negativity, but these are only acceptable for the time
that you give them. If they are valid reminiscence
of things you must resolve, do so. If they are just
memories with no resolution accept it as so and learn
to understand how to make peace with the same.
Holding onto those things that cannot find a place
will be a shadow in your dreams.

Recollection

Today she only sees the reflection of a time others gave her. She cannot recall a time of joy or happiness from the veil of silence that was a part of her life. The secrets held were prisons for all those within them. Today is the day she will take her life back and fight the shadow that allowed her to keep herself from living. The journey will be long and unrelenting at times, but a journey that must be taken to gain the distance needed from a time such as this.

Doors of yesterday

She was just a child when his visits began. It was a time when no child should ever bear. It is a time that she must work through and find a place in the history of her mind. It will never be forgotten. For one, such a time, only reminds her of the days she wishes she never saw. As a child she was unable to fight back, but today as her body has matured, she will find a way to never allow herself to be treated that way again. She still has many years for her mind to mature from the trauma she endured. For these adult children it is extremely hard fitting into a place others could never imagine. Never give up on finding that place for you. Don't allow those memories to control today.

Begin anew

When you wake and feel as if this day has nothing to offer you. You must reach deep within yourself and fight the want to give up. Not every day will or has been a focus of the years you wished you did not remember. Just know this will pass in time. You will once again have the will to walk out of the darkness, into the place that will bring you the peace you so deserve.

Growth

Our lives are more powerful because of others. We may or may not interact with others through our daily lives, yet each encounter gives us so many possibilities for growth. It's when we take a moment to welcome others into our lives that the willingness to hear the lessons can begin. It's so easy to get caught up in our own thoughts that we will not look beyond those things we find familiar. We must break away from our normal comfort zone to gain so much that this life has to offer.

Chaos

Sometimes I look at others for strength and courage during those moments of weakness in my world. We each need to find a safe place to rest from the chaos we move through each day. I do gain so much from those around me. It's the embrace of others through love or thought that can bring a different perspective from those I may have held. To walk alone is an unrestricted path yet at times some paths are meant to be traveled with others. Nuances of the unknown may then become visible.

Unknown

When we search for meaning in the meaningless, what are we really looking for? For some reason we need to have answers to all things. Sometimes there just aren't answers to the injustice of others. We may find explanations in the how or even a what, but the why may elude the rational. As much as I try to find answers to many things in life, I accept that there are a few situations when the truth may never be known. Life is filled with unknows. I try to understand many things. in life. to gain knowledge of where I have been and where I am going. Sometimes life doesn't allow an opportunity of insight, just more questions.